THIS BOOK BELONGS TO

....

MINECRAFT SECRETS & CHEATS: 2020
A CENTUM BOOK 978-1-913110-83-3
Published in Great Britain by Centum Books Ltd
This edition published 2019

1 3 5 7 9 10 8 6 4 2

Centum Books Ltd, 20 Devon Square, Newton Abbot, Devon, TQ12 2HR, UK
books@centumbooksltd.co.uk
CENTUM BOOKS Limited Reg. No. 07641486
A CIP catalogue record for this book is available from the British Library.
Printed in Poland.

centum

MINECRAFT
SECRETS & CHEATS
2020

CONTENTS

WHAT'S INSIDE?!

THINGS TO FIND

Loads of ideas on pages 10 and 34!

16 AMAZING BUILD IDEAS!
GET INSPIRATION HERE!

LOADS OF MINECRAFT PUZZLES!
Test your brain on pages 14, 24, 28 and 48!

50 THE BIG MINECRAFT QUIZ! Test your knowledge!

MINECRAFT DID YOU KNOW...?

What better way to start our celebration of Minecraft than with a collection of amazing facts about our favourite game!

The first official release of Minecraft was in late 2011, although early test versions were available a year or two before that. The game looked a little different back then and has regularly evolved through ongoing updates!

The first test version of Minecraft took under a week to make! Back then, it was called Cave Game, before its name changed to Minecraft: Order Of The Stone. And then, of course, to Minecraft!

The world record for the most time spent playing Minecraft was set by Mark Walls-Sawchuk. In June 2016, he played the game non-stop for 35 hours, 40 minutes and two seconds. He was raising money for charity (but was allowed toilet breaks!).

The original creator of Minecraft, Notch, used social media to see if anyone wanted to buy his company and the game when he'd had enough of working on it. Microsoft – makers of the Xbox consoles – paid him over two billion dollars just three months later!

If you want to understand what an enderman is saying, it's just English, but backwards! The noise of a ghast, meanwhile, is made by a cat!

At the end of 2018, the only video game to have sold more copies than

There's a Minecraft film in the works, although it's not expected until 2021 at the earliest. The producer of *The LEGO Movie* is working on the project, which is going to be released by Warner Bros (the studio behind the *Harry Potter* films!).

Minecraft spin-off games have been produced! Minecraft: Story Mode was the first, a series of adventures released across two seasons in the visual style of Minecraft. There was even a version you could play using Netflix as well! The second spin-off is the newer Minecraft Dungeons game, which can be played by up to four people.

Lots of schools use Minecraft! So much so that a special Education Edition of the game was made and is now available around the world.

Minecraft was a hit very quickly, and without having to spend money on advertising! It soon notched up one million sales in a few weeks (and that was just for the beta version)! People found out about the game by

Minecraft is Tetris. And that's been around since the 1980s! In all, over 150 million copies of Minecraft have been bought around the world.

Minecraft has been released on lots of formats, but not all of them are supported any more. Whilst you can play the game on the PlayStation 3, the PS Vita, the Xbox 360 and Nintendo WiiU, you can't get updates for those versions of the game any more. Nor can you get updates for the Apple TV and Raspberry Pi versions any more!

other people talking about it and recommending it. That word of mouth got stronger up to and following the official release of the first proper version.

The original default skin in Minecraft

was that of Steve. But in 2014, Mojang added Alex as well. Since then, you've been able to start a game as either character, one male, one female.

The most popular version of Minecraft is the Pocket Edition played on tablets and mobile phones.

There have been spin-off novels from the Minecraft world that have been officially endorsed by Mojang! Authors such as Max Brooks and Tracey Baptiste have written adventures like *The Island* and *The Crash*, which each take place in the Minecraft world!

Official Minecraft LEGO sets were first made available in 2012 after someone submitted the idea to LEGO at the end of 2011. There was enough interest and the idea was approved. The first set arrived later on in 2012.

Minecraft makes an appearance in the movie *Ready Player One*, which came out in 2018! In the film's opening scenes, you can clearly see a Minecraft planet. The game has also popped up in the likes of *The Simpsons* and an assortment of other videogames too!

The first ever MineCon official Minecraft convention was held in November 2011 in Las Vegas, USA. Can you believe they only had 4500 tickets available?! They were all snapped up by the end of October! The following year's MineCon was held at Disneyland Paris, and they've been an annual event since, moving online back in 2017 so that we could all watch, whether we had a ticket or not!

The actual size of blocks in the game is supposed to relate to real life. Well, sort of! One block is said to represent one metre cubed in the real world.

The problem with that is it would mean a chicken was, well, three feet tall! Nearly twice as tall as the average human. Yikes!

Some features get taken away from Minecraft over time. For instance, biomes such as Seasonal Forest, Shrubland and Tundra have been removed from the game. Even some of the sounds in the game have changed over time as Minecraft has evolved and improved more and more.

There are no plans at all for a separate Minecraft 2, although the question does come up from time to time. Instead, Mojang is focusing on continual updates to Minecraft. It tends to announce some of its biggest updates at each winter's MineCon convention.

SCAVENGER HUNT PART 1

Here is Part 1 of our Minecraft scavenger hunt. Can you track down and take a screenshot of EVERYTHING on our list? Challenge your friends to see who can get the most!

There are 101 items to find in total. Remember, everything has to be NATURALLY generated – stuff you craft or place doesn't count!

A desert well

Watch out for the patrol!

A flower forest

PART 1

EASY STUFF

1 point each

1 A desert well
2 Some mushrooms growing underground
3 A patrol of pillagers
4 A wild pumpkin patch
5 A flower forest
6 A full moon
7 A forest fire started by lava
8 A grass path
9 Sand that's ready to fall if you touch it
10 Water (or lava) dripping through the rocks above

LANDSCAPE FEATURES

5 points each

11 A lagoon on the coastline

12 A dust bowl where the soil has been stripped away on the side of a mountain

13 A cave that leads all the way through a mountain and out the other side

14 A mountain that rises above the clouds

15 A ravine that intersects with another ravine

16 An island with a single tree on it

17 A cave with a river flowing down it

18 A river that has mostly dried up

A surface mine

The rarest biome

Mountain above the clouds

An island with one tree

RARE STUFF

10 points each

19 A zombie wearing gold armour

20 Flowers growing in the entrance of an abandoned mine

21 A gold mine above ground in a Mesa biome

22 A dolphin swimming in a river

23 A village on the edge of a coastline

24 Zombies destroying turtle eggs

25 Some emerald ore

26 A Mushroom Island biome

GLITCHES

20 points each

27 A witch hut with extremely long legs

28 An igloo basement with broken walls

29 A chunk of land floating unsupported in the sky

30 A house on the side of a hill

31 A desert temple where the door is buried

32 A jungle temple in the middle of a lake

33 An abandoned mine that intersects another mine

34 A shipwreck that's completely out of the water

A block floating unsupported

A glitch village

COMMON PLANTS AND BLOCKS

1 point each

35 Red poppy

36 Yellow dandelion

37 Lilypad

38 Rose bush

39 Cornflower

40 Lily of the Valley

41 Coal ore

42 Iron ore

43 Ice

Cornflowers

Ice

LESS COMMON PLANTS AND BLOCKS

5 points each

44 Redstone ore
45 Iron ore
46 Lapis lazuli
47 Huge mushroom
48 Patch of sunflowers
49 Two different coloured tulips
50 Giant tree (can be dark oak, spruce or jungle tree)
51 Melon patch
52 Bamboo

Tulips

Dark oak trees

Bed

SUPER-RARE PLANTS AND BLOCKS

20 points each

62 Bone blocks (found as part of a fossil)
63 Damaged anvil (hint: search woodland mansions)
64 Blue ice
65 Tree whose leaves are discoloured from crossing biomes
66 Tall birch tree
67 Blocks of gold
68 Glazed terracotta

RARE PLANTS AND BLOCKS

10 points each

53 Diamond ore
54 Any loot chest
55 Packed ice
56 Acacia tree with a completely straight trunk
57 Small jungle tree
58 Sponge blocks
59 Carved sandstone
60 Bed
61 Banner

Diamond ore

Bone blocks

PUZZLE PAGES

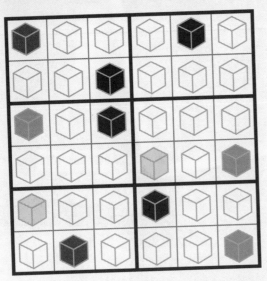
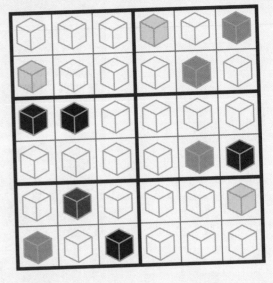
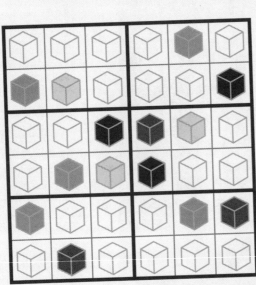
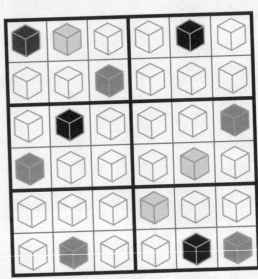

BLOCKDOKU

Iron   Red Sandstone   Ice   Obsidian   Emerald   Gold

Can you colour in the block grids above following three simple rules?
1) Each square must contain a block
2) Each of the red rectangles must contain all six kinds of block
3) No type of block can appear on any line twice, horizontally or vertically

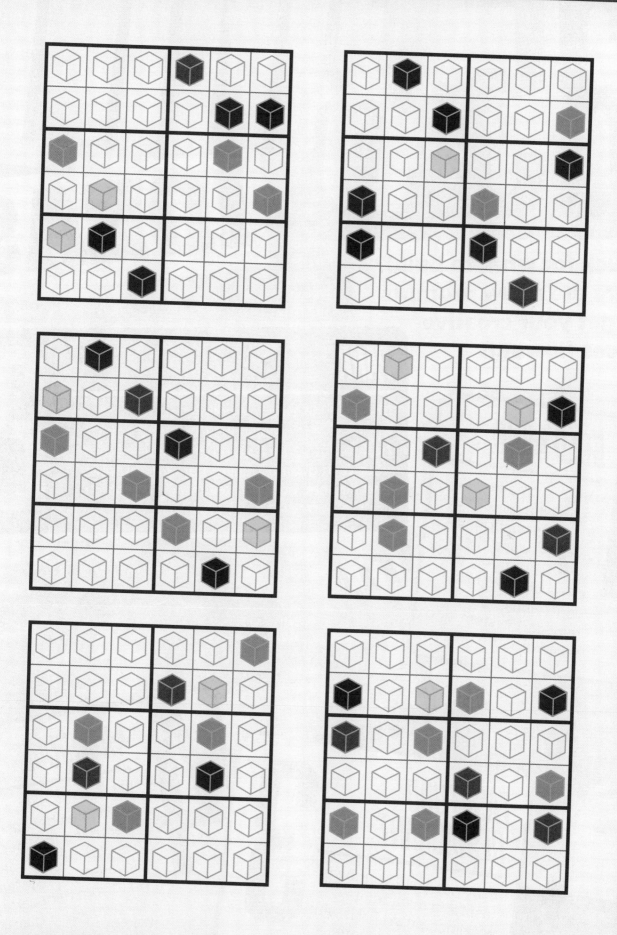

25 BUILD IDEAS

Stuck for what to build? Here are a few prompts to get your creative juices flowing!

PARK
2

The wild landscape of Minecraft is impressive in its own way, but why not flatten out some land and manicure it into your own quaint-looking park? Plant trees and flowers, build a duck pond and, of course, surround it with railings.

GOLD MINE
1

Why not make yourself a mine? You can find abandoned mines around the world, but rarely on the surface. Build yourself a cool minecart system, and fill it with rare ore!

FAST FOOD RESTAURANT
3

Why not build your own fast food restaurant – McMinecraft's?! Fill it with seating, add a counter, and you'll be flipping burgers in no time!

MONORAIL
4

It's not TECHNICALLY a monorail because everything in Minecraft has two rails, but an elevated train system built from minecarts will give you a quick way to travel with a fantastic view!

SHOP

5

Why not build a bakery or a fishmongers? Large glass windows, a till and some display racks are all easy to make in Minecraft.

SECRET BASE

9

Whether you make a secret high-tech basement accessed by a hatch or a hollowed-out hideaway in a mountain, there's no base better than the supervillain's choice – a secret base!

WATERWHEEL

6

Alternatively, if you want to keep things rural, find a tranquil river and add a waterwheel-powered mill at the water's edge. Build it out of wood for an authentic look.

GARDEN

10

What's a house without a garden? Surround it with bushes or a fence, add a patio and furniture, or a rustic bench and water feature – either way, you'll have the perfect place to relax outdoors.

BRIDGE

7

Sick of swimming awkwardly across rivers or hiking around lakes? An old-fashioned bridge – or a modern one! – is a great project to help you really put your stamp on the world.

FARM

11

Minecraft's typical farms are small and basic. Why not build a full-size one with a barn, farmhouse, fields of wheat and, of course, a field full of cattle? Ah, the simple life!

SWIMMING POOL

8

You can swim in the lakes, rivers and sea, but nothing beats your own pool. Line it with prismarine, light it with sea lanterns, and add your own diving board and Jacuzzi.

12 NETHER BASE

The Nether is an unforgiving place, so why not build your own safe haven there around your entry portal? It will make coming and going far, far less stressful!

13 WATER PARK

Nothing beats a water park for fun. Build water spouts, slides, boat races, a diving area and more to bring some water-world fun to Minecraft.

14 LIGHTHOUSE

Why are there so many shipwrecks in Minecraft? Probably because there are no lighthouses! Fix that by building some using redstone lamps and daylight sensors to automate them!

15 HENGE

Just as the Druids built Stonehenge, you can build your own henge in Minecraft to give an ancient, historical feel to your world. Add a portal or enchanting table for a mystical touch!

16 TREEHOUSE

Living on the ground is fine, but up in the trees is perhaps the safest place. No mobs are going to climb all the way up there without you spotting them!

17 ROLLERCOASTER

Life may be a rollercoaster, but an ACTUAL rollercoaster is a much better one. Use tracks and redstone-powered rails to speed a cart around your own twisty, turn-y track.

18 VOLCANO

Minecraft has plenty of mountains and lava but no volcanoes. Dig a crater in a hill, then combine it with a lava source and magma blocks for an active volcano look!

19 PIXELART CREATION

Minecraft's coloured blocks make the perfect palette for some pixelart, so why not stack them up to make your own creation based on Pokémon, Mario, or anything you like?

23 MAP WALL

Mapping large areas in Minecraft is fun, but why not display your maps as one huge map by filling a wall with item frames and placing the maps inside them so they join up?

20 A MODERN HOUSE

Fancy yourself as an architect? Why not design your perfect two (three, or four!) bedroom home? Furnishing each room in a way that looks real is a great little puzzle in itself!

24 THEME PARK

Want to entertain your friends? Why not build a theme park based around your favourite pop-culture icons? Make it a Minecraft-centric experience with escape rooms, mazes, jumping puzzles and more!

21 ZOO

Want to see all of Minecraft's animals in one place? Then it's up to you to house them. Build their habitats and populate your zoo with animals for people to come and visit. Don't forget to feed them!

22 SPHINX

There are plenty of deserts in Minecraft, and even the odd temple, but as fun as it is to build pyramids, your Egyptian-style monuments won't be complete without a Sphinx! It will look purr-fect!

25 JUNGLE PYRAMID

Clear out the jungle and use carved stone blocks to put up a Mayan-style stepped pyramid. Cover it with vines for an overgrown look, and don't forget the skeletons and treasure inside!

Looking for inspiration? Check out our huge collection of YouTubers and builds!

WEBSITES & YOUTUBERS!

YOUTUBERS

DanTDM
We couldn't leave out DanTDM when namechecking the best YouTubers around. He posts fewer Minecraft videos these days, but he still checks in with the community and goes on hilarious adventures with Doctor Trayaurus, who has almost become more of a well-known character than Dan at this point! With over 21 million subscribers now, Dan is simply unstoppable.
tinyurl.com/MC2020YT1

Mini Muka
If roleplay videos are your thing, then get ready to have some serious Minecraft fun with Muka!

Not only are his roleplay adventures epic, he does loads of live videos too. From making a secret base to running Noob Vs Pro diamond races, there will definitely be something to eat up your time on Muka's channel.
tinyurl.com/MC2020YT2

Preston
Preston is still posting the odd Minecraft video or two and they're always worth a look. Many of the more recent ones end up with him trolling his little brother, but to be fair the little guy does keep coming back for more! Preston's channel is all about getting the most fun possible out of games, Minecraft included!
tinyurl.com/MC2020YT3

CaptainSparklez
One of the biggest Minecraft YouTubers, CaptainSparklez is still going strong, making Minecraft music videos to pair with his own songs, and delighting just about everyone while doing it. Plenty of tips, tricks and extras are stuffed in-between the musical madness, so you'll not go wrong subscribing to this one!
tinyurl.com/MC2020YT4

MagmaMusen
MagmaMusen is a growing fave on YouTube, and it's not hard to see why. His family-friendly tutorials are easy to follow and tackle just about every little thing you could want to accomplish in Minecraft.

Want to make a DJ booth? Want to make a bubble bath? Want to make a goat? Yes, a goat! MagmaMusen is your one-stop tutorial shop.
tinyurl.com/MC2020YT5

Netty Plays

Indeed! Netty plays! Mainly Minecraft minigames and survival. She's just so watchable and easy to spend time with, which is good because she's one of the top live Minecraft queens of YouTube. Accompany Netty on the highs and lows of her adventures, and have fun playing minigames in real time with one of the loveliest in the biz.
tinyurl.com/MC2020YT6

Lextube

Minecraft Mods, Minecraft Let's Build, Timelapses, Modded Minecraft and more besides. Phew! Lextube tries to update seven days a week, so you'll always find something new and interesting to discover on his ever-popular channel. UK players will be overjoyed to see plenty of videos tailored to local interests here too.
tinyurl.com/MC2020YT7

Baby Duck

Baby Duck likes cookies. Oh, also Minecraft! If you want cookies, you're reading the wrong book. No recipes here. If you want crazy adventures, Baby Duck has it covered. Evil grannies, spooky vampire lairs and superheroes gone wrong, there's rarely a scenario that hasn't made the cut. There's always an evil "something" on the loose!
tinyurl.com/MC2020YT8

PixelDip

Really going the extra mile to weave wonderful stories with Minecraft, PixelDip doesn't upload videos as often as a lot of other YouTubers, but you know that when one pops up it's going to be worth the wait. Featuring story-based Minecraft videos to inspire and intrigue you, PixelDip will take you on adventures you never dreamed possible.
tinyurl.com/MC2020YT9

LDShadowLady

With around 5 million subscribers, Lizzie's Minecraft series are the ones to beat. Using mods like Minecraft One Life, Ultra Hardcore, Base Invaders and Shadowcraft, she always has something to reel you in. Once you've watched a few of her vids, it will be easy to see why she's one of the most incredible YouTubers around.
tinyurl.com/ MC2020YT10

BUILDS

Rose

Sometimes the simplest things keep us happy, and this beautiful rose is so sweet we can practically smell it. The creator built it as a test, and it only took a couple of hours using the Arceon Loft tool! Wonderful. Now, can we have a dozen, please?
tinyurl.com/MC2020B10

Buried Skeleton

Not much to do here except marvel in the magnificence of this enormous skeleton built into the earth like a giant, extinct humanoid alien creature that failed to survive an apocalyptic event. The crater terrain was constructed in World Machine, and the skeleton was made with the OMB plugin.
tinyurl.com/MC2020B9

Roses are red

Lazy bones!

Lord of
the manor

Sweets Island

An entire island good enough to eat – hard to imagine anything more delightful! Cakes, sweets, lollies and an oversized, mischievous puppy who wants to get a taste too. The colours and textures here caught our eye, and we can imagine having a brilliant time wandering around this build and getting a bit of a sugar rush.
tinyurl.com/MC2020B8

Bumblebee Vs Stinger

It's a giant Bumblebee and a giant Stinger

doing battle in Minecraft! Sure, they might bring down the city, but it would be worth it. A project worthy of the biggest Transformers fans out there, this is some pretty ambitious 3D art – hats off to the builder.
tinyurl.com/MC2020B7

Victorian Château

This Victorian château is not only finished from the outside, but also on the inside! The floral tessellations and the sandy colour aesthetic were inspired by

the theme of rose gold. Weirdly, this started off as a Disney horror mansion before being reimagined as this incredible château. It's funny how things work out.
tinyurl.com/MC2020B6

Verdigris Dragon

Another piece of 3D art that wowed us and left us reeling! The colouring and detail on the dragon's scales is out of this world. What a blinding project.
tinyurl.com/MC2020B5

Colourful Town

This took five months to build, and honestly it would have taken us at

Sweet as candy!

Autobots, roll out!

Fantastic beast!

Turning Japanese

least a year. The dedication to detail in this town is simply amazing. From the weird shapes to the vibrant colours, it just blew us away. A project that is brilliant, ambitious and full of joy all at once.
tinyurl.com/MC2020B4

Neon In The City Of Japan
An outstanding little build that gives us the feeling of being in the centre of Japan, with all its lights, billboards and surprises. Since it's quite expensive

to go there on holiday, we'll stick to this for now, and try to imagine what it would be like if Japan were made of big Minecraft blocks instead.
tinyurl.com/MC2020B3

Viking Longship
Available to download (and why would you not?), you can pretend to be a Viking with this stellar longship. The architect used the John Smith Legacy JSC texture pack for this one after apparently being inspired by the live-action *Vicky The Viking*

movie. Whatever led to its creation, we're on board – it's a knockout.
tinyurl.com/MC2020B2

Star Wars – The Battle Of Hoth
As Star Wars fans, we were amazed by this Hoth Battle diorama! It looks deceptively simple, but we can tell a lot of love and work has gone into this one. The wee TIE fighters! The ATSTs! Holy macaroni, this is superb. Tempted to build your own? You're not alone, we're feeling it too!
tinyurl.com/MC2020B1

All the colours of the rainbow

Row, row, row your boat

Use the force, Luke

PUZZLE PAGES

Can you spot the six changes we've made to the picture?

SPOT THE DIFFERENCE

MINECRAFTIFY

Can you name the nine delicious foods we've treated
to a Minecraft makeover?

One of the best ways to protect your base is to make sure no one even knows it's there – and to do that, you'll have to make a secret entrance! Here are a few ways you can do it...

HOW TO MAKE A SECRET

HIDDEN TREE ENTRANCE

If you're in a biome with larger trees, you can easily hide a doorway inside one! This is a little harder to do if the trees are slim, but dark oak and jungle trees are great for it! All you have to do is make the trunk three blocks wide and three blocks deep, then cut a hole in the middle, with a pit directly under the centre.

Now, add a door of whatever type blends into the wood best. You can further obscure its appearance by adding a thicket of flower bushes, large ferns, tall grass or whatever plant is common to the biome you're in!

UNDERWATER TUNNEL

If your base is near to deep water, you can add an underwater tunnel where you can get in and out without others finding it. The secret here is to make sure you can't see the entrance when you're on the surface of the water. The easiest way to

A tree entrance with its cover ferns removed

An underwater tunnel

An uncovered waterfall entrance

ENTRANCE

A painting from the inside

do this is to build a pipe jutting outwards, then make it so you can swim into it from below. Once the tunnel is built, make sure no light leaks out, and camouflage the top.

WATERFALL ENTRANCE

There are caves everywhere in Minecraft, and it's not unusual to see water springing from a mountainside. You can use these two facts to create a secret door to your base! Either find an existing water spring

Vines obscure an entrance

or embed a water source block above the place you want to make your entrance, then carve a small hole in the rock behind where it's flowing, ideally some way up the mountainside. If you do it correctly, the water will make it hard to see the entrance, then when you want to use it you can swim up the downward flowing water and slip inside your base without anyone realising!

INVISIBLE DOORWAY

The simplest of secret entrances: build an S-shaped passage into a hill near your base. The bend will make it impossible to see the door from the outside no matter what angle you're looking at it from. The larger you make the passage,

the easier it will be to hide, and it can help to put vines, tall plants or sugar cane in front so it's even harder to make out. Again, keep light sources far away!

PAINTING DOOR

A fairly simple but impressive secret door: craft a 2x1 tunnel, then place two signs, one on top of the other, in the space. Place a painting on the wall to the bottom left of the passage and it will cover up the whole thing (assuming there's space). You can then run in and out without anyone else knowing that's how you did it. Genius!

27

PUZZLE PAGES

Can you spot the six changes we've made to the picture?

SPOT THE DIFFERENCE

WORDSEARCH

Can you pick out the 21 chunks of Minecraft miscellany
hidden in this letter grid?

H	E	R	O	B	R	I	N	E	P	J	P	M	N	Z	C	S	Z	T	L
A	N	I	I	M	V	E	R	N	R	E	D	S	T	O	N	E	O	R	E
V	S	F	B	B	T	U	N	D	R	A	A	R	K	M	Y	S	D	G	J
F	P	C	S	B	B	B	B	E	R	E	Q	G	D	B	A	V	I	E	B
N	O	T	S	I	L	V	E	R	F	I	S	H	U	I	M	W	D	J	L
M	N	D	N	L	C	P	T	P	Z	D	M	A	O	E	J	I	C	K	C
K	G	O	R	M	T	G	C	E	B	Y	G	S	O	P	U	T	O	Z	H
O	E	N	Q	A	U	C	V	A	A	F	I	T	P	I	Y	H	X	J	A
J	D	A	W	S	G	I	S	R	H	W	T	E	C	G	L	E	I	M	I
P	O	V	E	R	W	O	R	L	D	N	Y	V	H	M	G	R	U	I	N
U	L	H	K	T	D	O	N	B	K	X	A	H	O	A	F	S	H	N	M
P	P	W	E	R	F	P	L	E	B	O	L	Z	R	N	G	K	P	F	A
T	H	T	U	B	M	K	L	V	G	I	R	Q	U	O	P	E	W	O	I
R	I	C	P	L	M	V	G	H	E	G	B	O	S	K	N	L	O	K	L
D	N	S	T	U	I	J	S	Z	L	S	H	I	P	W	R	E	C	K	A
C	D	Z	V	R	E	T	A	Q	T	W	U	M	L	E	T	T	D	X	R
Y	E	M	E	R	A	L	D	A	F	N	X	D	A	S	U	O	V	S	M
I	O	P	X	C	B	Q	R	P	E	C	W	B	N	C	T	N	U	I	O
L	G	H	P	M	D	L	O	H	G	N	O	R	T	S	M	K	Q	J	U
K	R	Y	L	V	G	P	N	E	T	H	E	R	S	T	A	R	W	A	R

Blaze	Emerald	Overworld	Sponge
Chainmail Armour	Ender Pearl	Redstone Ore	Stronghold
Chorus Plants	Ghast	Ruin	Tundra
Dolphin	Herobrine	Shipwreck	Wither Skeleton
Dragon Egg	Nether Star	Silverfish	Wolves
			Zombie Pigman

THE COMPLETE LOOT AND TREASURE GUIDE

Minecraft is full of riches, often found in chests dotted around the world! If you're after something specific, learn where to search!

All of these item lists are ordered from the most common to the most rare. Remember that chests contain a random selection of items from the lists given, not EVERYTHING! While there is some crossover in the items you can find, some chests have items that can't be found in other types of chest, so watch out for those!

BONUS CHESTS

A bonus chest is generated at the spawn point if you tick the box during world generation. It contains loot that's useful early on: sticks, oak planks, apples, raw salmon, bread, wooden pickaxe, wooden axe, spruce log, oak log, jungle log, dark oak log, birch log, acacia log, stone pickaxe and stone axe.

BURIED TREASURE

Buried treasure can be found under the sea floor using maps or by following friendly dolphins. They contain super-valuable items: iron ingots, gold ingots, emeralds, cooked salmon, cooked cod, prismarine crystals, TNT, diamonds, a heart of the sea, iron swords and leather tunics.

IGLOOS

If an igloo has a hidden basement, you'll find a chest containing any of coal, apples, wheat, gold nuggets, golden apples, rotten flesh, stone axes and emeralds.

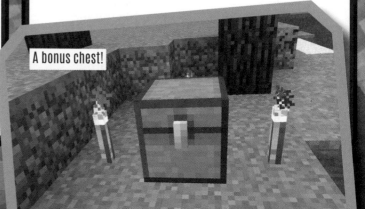

A bonus chest!

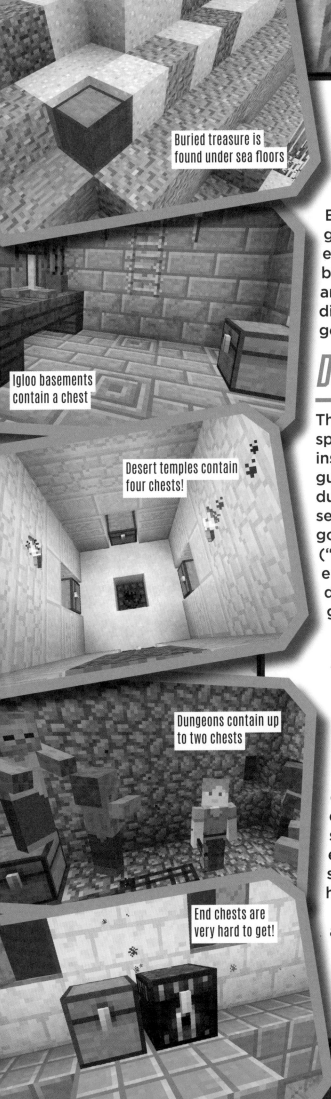

Buried treasure is found under sea floors

Igloo basements contain a chest

Desert temples contain four chests!

Dungeons contain up to two chests

End chests are very hard to get!

DESERT TEMPLES

If you find a desert temple, you're in luck as they contain four chests! The loot isn't very unique, but at least there's a lot of it! Each chest can contain bones, rotten flesh, gunpowder, sand, string, gold ingots, spider eyes, iron ingots, emeralds, enchanted books, saddles, golden apples, iron horse armour, golden horse armour, diamonds, diamond horse armour and enchanted golden apples.

DUNGEONS

These small chambers containing monster spawners can have up to two chests. The loot inside is a selection of bones, rotten flesh, gunpowder, string, wheat, coal, redstone dust, beetroot seeds, melon seeds, pumpkin seeds, iron ingots, bread, name tags, saddles, gold ingots, golden apples, music discs ("13" or "Cat"), buckets, iron horse armour, enchanted books, gold horse armour, diamond horse armour and enchanted golden apples.

END CITIES

The chests in End cities are very hard to get to and only accessible very late in the game, so they have the best loot by far. You can expect to see gold ingots, iron ingots, beetroot seeds, diamonds, emeralds, enchanted diamond armour (all pieces), enchanted diamond pickaxes, shovels and swords, enchanted iron armour (all pieces), enchanted iron pickaxes, shovels and swords, saddles, iron horse armour, golden horse armour and diamond horse armour.

The enchantments on enchanted items are usually very high – the same as you'd receive for a Level 39 enchantment, which is higher than it's possible to even make using an enchantment table (they're capped at Level 30!).

Jungle temple have visible and hidden chests

Look out for abandoned chest minecarts

Shipwrecks have three types of chest

Ruins have large or small chests

JUNGLE TEMPLES

Jungle temples have two chests: one visible, one hidden. The loot in both contains bones, rotten flesh, gold ingots, iron ingots, diamonds, emeralds, saddles, iron horse armour, gold horse armour, diamond horse armour and enchanted books.

ABANDONED MINES

In abandoned mines, you'll occasionally find abandoned chest minecarts. These act the same as normal treasure chests and contain torches, rails, coal, lapis lazuli, redstone, bread, iron ingots, beetroot seeds, melon seeds, pumpkin seeds, activator rails, detector rails, powered rails, name tags, gold ingots, golden apples, diamonds, enchanted books, iron pickaxes and enchanted golden apples.

SHIPWRECKS

There are three types of chest in a shipwreck: **Map chests** contain paper, feathers, books, buried treasure maps, empty maps, compasses and clocks.

Supply chests contain wheat, rotten flesh, paper, carrot, coal, potato, poisonous potato, gunpowder, pumpkin, enchanted leather clothes (all pieces) and TNT.

Treasure chests contain iron nuggets, iron ingots, lapis lazuli, emerald, gold nuggets, gold ingots, bottle o' enchanting and diamonds.

RUINS

Underwater ruins have two variants depending on whether the ruin is large or small. Large ones contain coal, wheat, gold nuggets, buried treasure maps, enchanted books, enchanted fishing rods, emeralds, golden apples, golden helmets and leather tunics. Small ones don't have gold items or enchanted books, and instead contain rotten flesh and a stone axe.

NETHER FORTRESSES

Chests in the Nether have lots of great loot, which is no surprise given how hard it is to get it home safely! You can find gold ingots, Nether wart, iron ingots, diamonds, saddles, gold horse armour, obsidian, iron horse armour, flint and steel, golden chestplate, golden sword and diamond horse armour.

Nether fortress chests contain cool loot!

Strongholds contain a lot of chests!

STRONGHOLDS

The size of strongholds means there are lots of items to find and three different types of chest, depending on the rooms in the stronghold. You can expect to find a good number of chests in any stronghold you visit!

Altar chests contain redstone, bread, iron ingots, apples, gold ingots, ender pearls, diamonds, iron pickaxes, iron armour (all pieces), iron swords, golden apples, saddles, diamond horse armour, gold horse armour, iron horse armour and enchanted books.

In libraries, the chests contain just a few items, but they're very uncommon: paper,

books, enchanted books, compasses and empty maps.

Finally, storeroom chests can contain coal, redstone, bread, iron ingots, apples, gold ingots, enchanted books and iron pickaxes.

WOODLAND MANSIONS

These huge, mysterious buildings can contain chests in a number of spots, but each one has the same chance of containing the same items: gunpowder, string, bone, rotten flesh, wheat, coal, redstone dust, pumpkin seeds, melon seeds, beetroot seeds, iron ingots, bread, leads, name tags, gold ingots, diamond hoes, music discs ("Cat" and "13"), golden apples, buckets, chainmail chestplate, enchanted books, diamond chestplates and enchanted golden apples.

Woodland mansions contain a number of chests

SCAVENGER HUNT PART 2

Now try Part 2 of our giant scavenger hunt! Can you track down and take a screenshot of EVERYTHING on our list? There are 101 items to find in total. This time, they're themed on the Nether and the End. Remember they have to be NATURALLY generated – stuff you craft or place doesn't count! Good luck!

The End

Soul sand

I point each

COMMON NETHER/THE END STUFF

69 End stone
70 Netherrack
71 Brown mushroom
72 Red mushroom
73 Soul sand
74 Glowstone
75 Zombie pigman
76 Blaze
77 Nether wart
78 Inactive exit portal

An inactive portal

LESS COMMON NETHER/THE END STUFF

5 points each

79 Iron railings
80 Chorus plant
81 Gravel
82 Nether quartz ore
83 Ghast
84 Wither skeleton
85 Bedrock
86 Nether bricks

Chorus plants

Nether bedrock

A ghast. Terrifying!

Purpur blocks

Magma blocks

End rods

RARE NETHER/ THE END STUFF

87 Purpur blocks
88 Purpur pillars
89 End stone bricks
90 Magma blocks
91 Endermen
92 (Non-wither) skeleton
93 Loot chest
94 End rods

SUPER-RARE NETHER/THE END STUFF

20 points each

95 Dragon's head
96 Elytra in an item frame
97 Mob spawner
98 Magma cubes
99 Active exit portal
100 Purple and black banners
101 Purple stained glass blocks

A dragon head

Elytra in a frame

An active portal

It you want to create an amazing Minecraft build, it makes sense to take a bit of time planning it first! It's worth sketching out your idea and finding any problems before you head to the game. Plus, if you have something to refer to, it tends to make things easier!

PLANNING A BRILLIANT MINECRAFT BUILD!

On the right, you'll find a sheet of planning paper for you to draw your build on. But before you get out your pencils, consider the following:

☐ Is it just your building, or are you working with friends/siblings? If others are involved, make them part of the planning process, then divide up the work between you!

☐ Start small! If it's one of your first builds, focus on building a small house and on making it as brilliant as possible.

☐ Do the edges and the corners first! Then you can gradually fill in your build from the outside in.

☐ Save the details for later! For now, just get the basic structure in place. You can decorate it once you've finished!

☐ Don't be afraid to rub it all out and start again! Sometimes a good idea just doesn't work out. It happens to us all and is part of the fun of putting together a Minecraft build!

FURNITURE MINI-BUILDS

Kitting out your base is always a fun way to spend time, so here are a few of our favourite furniture mini-builds to give you that polished look in minutes!

Relax after a busy day...

Impress with this clock

BATHTUB

You need: **Trapdoors, buckets of water, tripwire hooks**
Place the trapdoors (birch ones look best, but you can use any kind) on the floor, then open them so they stand up to create the edge of the bath. Fill the inside with water and use tripwire hooks as "taps".

GRANDFATHER CLOCK

You need: **Dark oak bark, item frames, shovel, stick, clock**
Use bark blocks to build a tall post, then, using item frames, attach a clock face to the top. Put a stick in the middle and a shovel below to look like a pendulum – you'll have to rotate them both to line up!

FIREPLACE

You need: **Slabs, iron bars, paintings, plant pots, flowers, Netherrack, flint and steel**
A fireplace will brighten up any room. Use slabs to build the frame, and place railings in front as a fire guard. Netherrack burns forever, so use that as the "fuel"!

Create a cosy look

Add a pop of colour!

Create some mood lighting

FLOOR LAMP

You need: **End rods, plant pot**
Stack two End rods on top of each other, then put a plant pot on the top to look like a lampshade. The End rods will be emitting the light, but it looks like a free-standing floor lamp!

CURTAINS

You need: **Banners**
Fairly simple: just attach two banners to the top of a window to create a pair of curtains – they'll attach to glass panes without any problem!

DESK LAMP

You need: **Sea lantern, trapdoors, fence post**
Surround a sea lantern (or any glowing block) with trapdoors (except on the bottom) and place a fence post underneath to create a desk lamp.

Place it on your desk...

COMPUTER

You need: **Stairs, activator rail, painting**
Stick a painting to the back of any stair block to act as the screen, and an activator rail in front to be the "keyboard".

Just need a coffee table now

...next to your computer

SOFA

You need: **Stairs, trapdoors**
To make a sofa, put two stair blocks next to one another, then put trapdoors at either end so that when you open them they sit alongside the blocks to form armrests.

Make your room look more alive

DOUBLE BED

You need:
Any two beds
There's no secret to this one – to make a double-sized bed, you can easily place two beds right next to one another and they'll look perfect.

PLANTER

You need:
Dirt, trapdoors, a plant
Surround a dirt block with trapdoors, then open them to create a large wooden planter. Now put in your plant!

Loads of room for two!

OUTDOOR MINI-BUILDS

Filled your base and want to start landscaping the world around it? Here are a few more mini-builds to make your world look awesome without taking forever to craft!

GRAVE

You need: Sign, polished andesite, torch, chests
Dig two blocks down and two across, and place a double chest in the open pit for a "coffin". Cover it with andesite, then use another andesite block with a torch and sign attached as the headstone. You can write anyone's name you like.

Spooooky!

PATIO SET

You need: Quartz stairs, carpet, fence posts, sandstone, slabs
Make your furniture white to resemble garden furniture. A checkerboard pattern made using sandstone and stone slabs will look better than a single design on its own.

Anyone for a quick dip?

HOT TUB

You need: Lava, water, glass blocks, stairs, levers
Dig down two blocks and place some lava blocks in the bottom of your pit. Cover them with glass blocks to make a see-through floor, then surround that with stairs. Fill the inside with water, then attach levers nearby to look like water taps. Voilà: one heated pool!

OLD WELL

You need: Mossy cobblestone wall, cobblestone wall, cobblestone stairs, iron bar, mossy cobblestone, water

Dig a deep pit one block wide, then line the edge with mossy cobblestone. Fill it with water, then put a mossy wall around it. Use wall posts at each corner to support the "roof" made of stairs. Finally, hang an iron bar from the centre to look like a bucket lowering in.

Perfect for a medieval village build

SPOOKY GATES

You need: Iron bars, spruce doors, torches, stone blocks

Building gates this way, with high gateposts and iron railings, makes them look more imposing – perfect for graveyards, haunted houses or old mansions.

MARKET

You need: Oak logs, stairs, oak planks, chests

Why not create a small market-style shop? Build a frame using oak, then add a roof and a back wall. Put counters alongside chests for shoppers to browse. Display cakes, plants, or any other placeable item.

These are pretty impressive gates

Who would you have as a statue?

STATUE

You need: Slabs, armour, armour stand, mob head

Build a plinth using slabs, put an armour stand on top, then hang the armour and head on the stand. You can swap one of the slabs for a sign if you want space to explain who the statue is!

SEWER

You need: Ladder, trapdoor, mossy stone bricks

Carve out the area under your streets to build a network of sewers! Use just one source block so the water looks like it's flowing, and mossy stone bricks for that damp look. Use a ladder with a trapdoor for a manhole cover.

PARK

You need: Gravel, flowers, lily pads, stairs, iron bars, water, tree

Fence off an area using iron bars as railings, then add a gravel path. Put in a pond and stairs for a bench, then decorate with flowers and a tree. Now you can relax in your own park!

10 GAMES TO PLAY IN MULTIPLAYER MODE

Want to play AGAINST your pals rather than alongside them? Here are 10 competition-style minigames! Set the game to Peaceful for the best results.

DEATHMATCH

The only rule here is the last one standing wins! It's a group fight to the death, where only one person can succeed. Keep your inventory safe in a chest!

TAG

Set a time limit and fence off an area, then keep track of who's "it". Whoever's tagged when the time limit runs out loses, and the next round continues without them.

HIDE & SEEK

Agree on a place to hide (this is good fun in villages and

Invite other players to deathmatch with them

mansions!), then one player has to try to find the others. You could also do it so that players who are found join in the search, to make the game shorter and more fun!

CAPTURE THE FLAG

Divide your group into two teams, each with their own single banner. Your goal is to capture the opponent's banner and bring it home while protecting your own! Hint: keep some spares in case your flag is destroyed or lost.

Shhhh, keep hidden

TARGET PRACTICE

Build a circular target 50 blocks away using coloured blocks – it can be upright or on the ground – then take turns firing three arrows from the 50-block line to see who can get them closest to the bullseye.

BOXING

Craft a small arena, drop all your weapons, armour and other combat items, then fight to the death using only your melee fists. The secret is to dodge and weave while going on the offensive.

FOOTRACE

Choose a landmark far away in the distance and see who can reach it first. Try to take different routes, otherwise it won't be as much fun! Boats, horses and vehicles are not allowed!

Capturing the flag is only half the fight!

SWIMMING RACE

Unlike walking, it takes skill to swim properly in Minecraft, so why not have a race across a lake or ocean? Manage your oxygen, avoid threats, or get a speed boost from a dolphin!

Build a target!

HIGH DIVE

Build a high dive board and jump off into a pool below. Next go, make the pool a bit smaller, and see if you can make it again. Repeat until the target is a single block of water or everyone loses their life...

Put your fists up

SCAVENGER RACE

A scavenger hunt where one person chooses a block type and every other player has to run out and find it. The last person to return with the block (or item) picks next time.

Have you ever tried to survive on an island with virtually no chance of escape? Well, if not, now's your chance with our survival island challenge!

PART ONE: SETTING THE SCENE

Starting the challenge is simple: begin a new world where you start the game on an island surrounded by sea. You can use a pre-discovered seed or just keep trying out new seeds until you get an island. It's worth keeping a note of the seed you're using because you'll then be able to play the challenge against your friends and see who does it best!

The island can be any size and have any amount of resources on it, but here's the catch: you can only use what you find on the island to stay alive. That means food, resources and space are all limited. And how limited they are determines how difficult your challenge is...

Survival islands have few resources

This island has tonnes of trees!

A classic simple survival island

SURVIVAL ISLAND CHALLENGE

PART TWO: PICKING A CHALLENGE

There are lots of ways to play your survival island challenge. Here are some variants:

■ Survival Island Classic

For this challenge, all you have to do is stay alive. Sounds simple, right? Well, not when there's no food around! The goal is to live for as long as possible, which means feeding yourself well and protecting yourself against mobs. It's just like playing Minecraft, only you can't wander very far! Remember to count each morning – perhaps use the console to give yourself a book to write tally marks in, or come up with a counting system using blocks. The longer you live, the better!

■ Escape Challenge

We know we said you can't leave, but for this version of the challenge you're encouraged to! The trick here is that you have to do it quickly and you have to survive until you reach the mainland (which sounds easier than it is!). The easiest way is to build a boat, in which case you need to hope you don't get attacked on the way off the island. But you can also make the challenge a lot harder by agreeing that you have to build, dig or swim your way off!

■ Full Armour Challenge

With limited resources, how long will it take to build a full set of armour? Level 1 of the challenge is iron, Level 2 is gold, and Level 3 is diamond! This is great for multiplayer, where you can have a back-and-forth fight over the resources on a given island, where you don't have to just find the necessary materials – you also have to try and keep them safe!

■ Portal Challenge

If you can't escape the island in the Overworld, how about escaping to the Nether? This is a super-fun way to play a survival island where your only goal is to stay alive long enough to build a portal and disappear into the Nether. Extend the challenge by making your goal to reach the mainland through a return portal!

Could you escape?

It's tough to get to the Nether

Who knows what you'll find?!

PUZZLE PAGES

Can you spot the seven changes we've made to the picture?

SPOT THE DIFFERENCE

BLOCK MAZE

Can you find the centre of our maze and bag the emerald?

Start here!

THE BIG MINECRAFT QUIZ!

Reckon you know your way around Minecraft? Take our quiz, and see how you measure up at the end!

1 IN WHAT YEAR WAS THE FIRST VERSION OF MINECRAFT OFFICIALLY RELEASED?

A 2005
B 2008
C 2011

2 WHICH OF THESE IS NOT A MOB IN MINECRAFT?

A Zombie pigman
B Turtle
C Owl

3 WHERE WILL YOU FIND THE ENDER DRAGON?

A The Start
B The Middle
C The End

4 WHAT DO YOU NEED TO POWER ITEMS IN MINECRAFT?

A Redstone
B Gas
C Wind

5 WITH WHICH OF THESE CAN YOU TRADE IN MINECRAFT?

A A skeleton
B A villager
C An ocelot

6 HOW BIG IS THE GRID IF YOU USE A CRAFTING TABLE TO CRAFT?
A 2x2
B 3x3
C 4x4

7 WHAT'S THE NAME OF THE ANNUAL ONLINE MINECRAFT CONVENTION?
A Minecon World
B Minecon Earth
C Minecon Global

8 WHICH OF THESE WAS AN ORIGINAL NAME FOR MINECRAFT?
A Blockbusters
B Cave Game
C Brickz

9 WHAT DO YOU NEED TO MAKE AN IRON GOLEM?
A Iron and pumpkin
B Iron and blue dye
C Iron and poisonous potato

10 WHICH OF THESE WAS THE NAME OF A MINECRAFT UPDATE?
A Update Gigantic
B Update Fantastic
C Update Aquatic

ANSWERS

1 C
2 C
3 C
4 A
5 B
6 B
7 B
8 B
9 A
10 C

HOW DID YOU DO?!

10: Wow! You're an absolute Minecraft expert. We're in awe!

8-9: You're an experienced Minecrafter and clearly know your way around the game!

6-7: You know lots about Minecraft, but we think there may still be a few things you don't know!

4-5: Not bad, but there's much in the world of Minecraft for you to discover!

0-3: Not to worry! You've now got a perfect excuse to learn even more about our favourite game!

ANSWERS

BLOCKDOKU (P14)

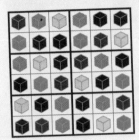
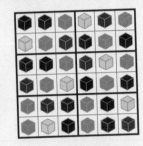
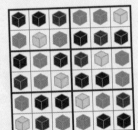
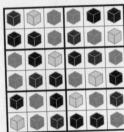

SPOT THE DIFFERENCE (P24)

BLOCKDOKU (P15)

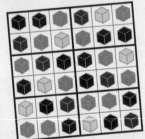
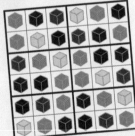
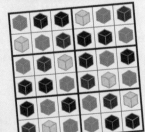
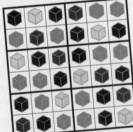
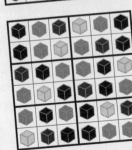
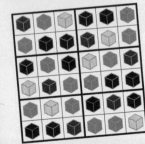

MINECRAFTIFY(P25)

SPOT THE DIFFERENCE (P28)

SPOT THE DIFFERENCE (P48)

WORDSEARCH (P29)

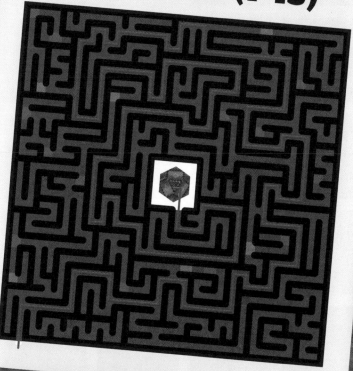

BLOCK MAZE (P49)

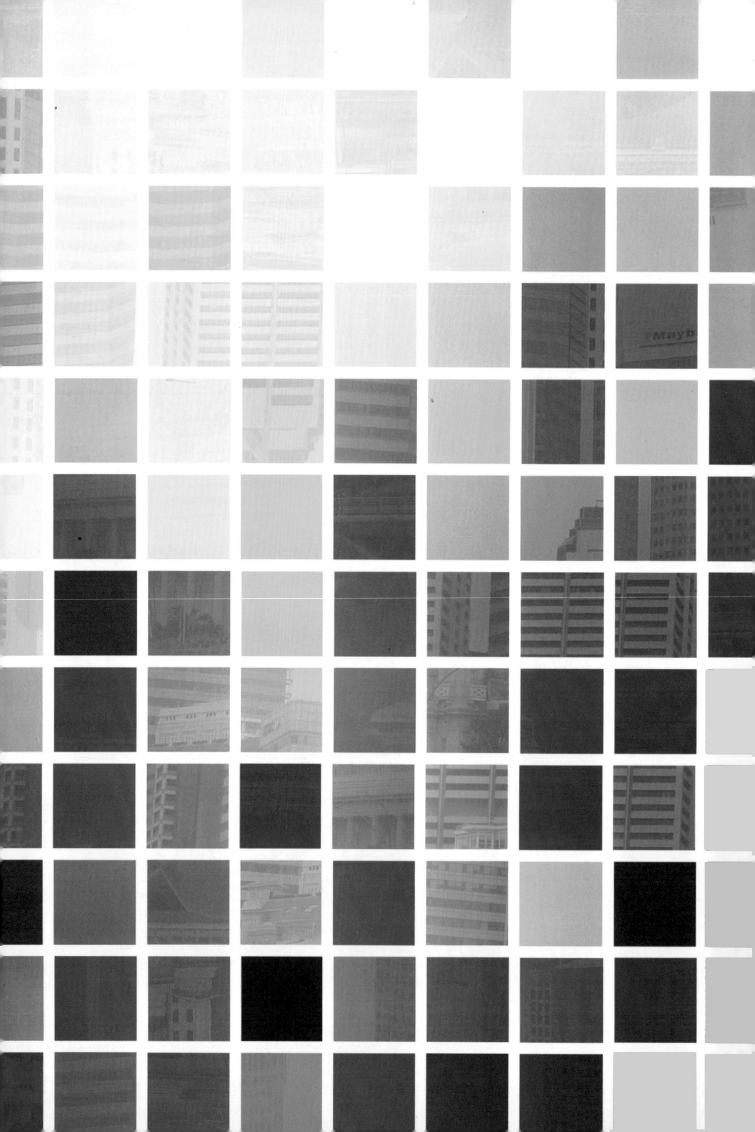